S0-ARJ-415

# Mark Messier

# Additional Titles in the Sports Reports *Series*

**Andre Agassi**
Star Tennis Player
(0-89490-798-0)

**Cal Ripken Jr.**
Star Shortstop
(0-89490-485-X)

**Troy Aikman**
Star Quarterback
(0-89490-927-4)

**David Robinson**
Star Center
(0-89490-483-3)

**Charles Barkley**
Star Forward
(0-89490-655-0)

**Barry Sanders**
Star Running Back
(0-89490-484-1)

**Ken Griffey, Jr.**
Star Outfielder
(0-89490-802-2)

**Deion Sanders**
Star Athlete
(0-89490-652-6)

**Michael Jordan**
Star Guard
(0-89490-482-5)

**Junior Seau**
Star Linebacker
(0-89490-800-6)

**Jim Kelly**
Star Quarterback
(0-89490-446-9)

**Emmitt Smith**
Star Running Back
(0-89490-653-4)

**Chris Mullin**
Star Forward
(0-89490-486-8)

**Frank Thomas**
Star First Baseman
(0-89490-659-3)

**Hakeem Olajuwon**
Star Center
(0-89490-803-0)

**Thurman Thomas**
Star Running Back
(0-89490-445-0)

**Shaquille O'Neal**
Star Center
(0-89490-656-9)

**Chris Webber**
Star Forward
(0-89490-799-9)

**Steve Young**
Star Quarterback
(0-89490-654-2)

SPORTS REPORTS

# Mark Messier

## Star Center

Michael J. Sullivan

**Enslow Publishers, Inc.**

| | |
|---|---|
| 40 Industrial Road | PO Box 38 |
| Box 398 | Aldershot |
| Berkeley Heights, NJ 07922 | Hants GU12 6BP |
| USA | UK |

http://www.enslow.com

Copyright © 1997 by Michael J. Sullivan

All rights reserved.

No part of this book may be reproduced by any means
without the written permission of the publisher.

**Library of Congress Cataloging-in-Publication Data**

Sullivan, Michael John, 1960–
     Mark Messier: star center / Michael J. Sullivan.
        p. cm. — (Sports reports)
     Includes bibliographical references and index.
     Summary: Presents a biography of the professional hockey player who has
led both the Edmonton Oilers and the New York Rangers to Stanley Cup
victories.
     ISBN 0-89490-801-4
     1. Messier, Mark, 1961– —Juvenile literature. 2. Hockey players—Canada—
Biography—Juvenile literature. [1. Messier, Mark, 1961– . 2. Hockey players.]
I. Title. II. Series.
GV848.5.M47S85 1997
796.962'092—dc21
[B]                                        96-52295
                                              CIP
                                              AC

Printed in the United States of America

10 9 8 7 6 5 4 3

**To Our Readers:** All Internet Addresses in this book were active and appropriate
when we went to press. Any comments or suggestions can be sent by e-mail to
Comments@enslow.com or to the address on the back cover.

**Illustration Credits:** AP/Wide World Photos, pp. 9, 11, 17, 23, 27, 34, 41, 44,
46, 56, 62, 65, 69, 74, 82, 87, 89, 91.

**Cover Illustration:** AP/Wide World Photos.

# Contents

**1** The Guarantee . . . . . . . . . . . . . . . . 7

**2** The Young Star . . . . . . . . . . . . . . . 21

**3** Winning the Cup . . . . . . . . . . . . . . 37

**4** The Captain . . . . . . . . . . . . . . . . 53

**5** Leading the Rangers . . . . . . . . . . . 67

**6** The Reunion . . . . . . . . . . . . . . . . 85

Chapter Notes . . . . . . . . . . . . . . 95

Career Statistics . . . . . . . . . . . . 99

Where to Write . . . . . . . . . . . . . 101

Index . . . . . . . . . . . . . . . . . . 102

# Chapter 1

# The Guarantee

The *New York Post* headline on May 25, 1994, shouted the unthinkable. Pasted on the back page of the daily sports section was the anguished unshaven face of Mark Messier, the captain of the New York Rangers. In big white letters on a dark background were the words of Captain Courageous: WE'LL WIN TONIGHT.

Was Messier boasting? Was he too confident? Was he putting more pressure on his teammates by guaranteeing a victory in the Stanley Cup Semifinals? After all, the Rangers were trailing the New Jersey Devils in the best-of-seven games series, 3-2. New York had just been beaten badly on its home ice at Madison Square Garden two nights earlier, in Game 5.

It was obvious that Messier was putting more pressure on his teammates, but he was also putting plenty of pressure on his own shoulders. He likes it that way. It wasn't unusual that Messier would be confident in rallying his team to victory, but athletes rarely make a confident cry for the public to read in the newspapers.

Game 6 was going to be tough to win for the Rangers because they were playing in front of the New Jersey fans this time. Their cross-river rivals have always given the Rangers a hard time, no matter where they played. A crowd of close to twenty thousand people jammed the Meadowlands Arena in East Rutherford, New Jersey. There were a few thousand Rangers fans in the stands, as there always were when these two teams played in New Jersey.

The crowd was roaring for the Devils from the opening face-off, and for good reason. New Jersey fans sensed that if the Devils got off to a fast start, they would bury the Rangers early. The Devils quickly attacked in the early moments of the first period. Bernie Nicholls, New Jersey's forward, moved in on a two-on-one advantage on Rangers goalie Mike Richter. Nicholls was about thirty-five feet to the right of Richter. He wound up to try a slap shot. The puck whizzed toward Richter, who just

*The race is on, as the Devils' Claude Lemieux tries to chase down Mark Messier.*

stuck up his arm to deflect the shot above the net. The crowd groaned.

The action continued to be fast and furious. Richter was forced to stop several New Jersey scoring opportunities. But the pressure by the Devils was bound to create a goal. Finally, it did. Devils defenseman Scott Niedermayer received a pass at a sharp angle to Richter's left side. Niedermayer, looking to find a teammate crossing in front of the net, threw a pass about three feet directly across from Richter. Rangers forward Sergei Nemchinov moved to intercept the pass and directed his stick in front of the puck. But he didn't stop the puck. Nemchinov deflected the puck in the air and toward the net. It went past Richter's right arm and into the net. New Jersey led, 1-0.

The Devils fans roared and screamed louder when some rock music was played, as their beloved team members congratulated each other for their hard work. The Rangers' offensive pressure was mild in comparison. New Jersey was clearly the best team so far in the first period, and it was clear that Mark Messier was going to have to do a lot more to back up his words.

It appeared that New Jersey wasn't listening. Devils goalie Martin Brodeur stopped consecutive shots by Messier, defenseman Brian Leetch, and

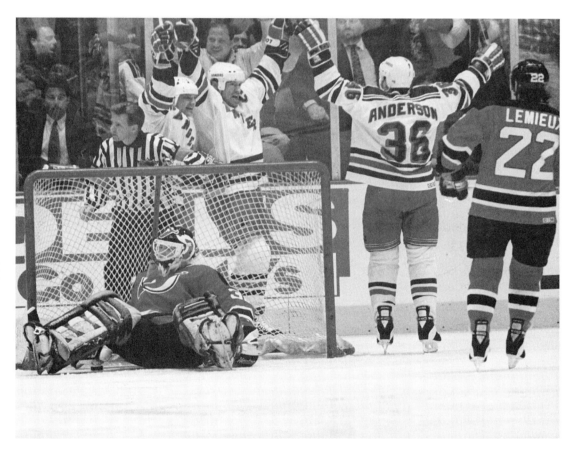

*Messier, center, celebrates a goal with teammates Esa Tikkanen, left, and Glenn Anderson, right, during Game 2 of the 1994 Eastern Conference Finals. The Devils, however, would lead the series 3-2 going into Game 6.*

forward Steve Larmer. The Devils were able to stop a Rangers power play. (This happens when a team is penalized for an infraction, and a player on that team has to sit in the penalty box for at least two minutes.)

As the crowd cheered the defensive work by the Devils, referee Kerry Fraser raised his arm to show that he was about to call a penalty on the Rangers. New York would have to gain possession of the puck for the play to stop. Then the Rangers player who had been called for the penalty would have to sit in the box for two minutes. But the Devils' Nicholls grabbed the puck in the corner to the right of Richter. He threaded a pass through a couple of players to Niedermayer, who was stationed about forty-five feet from the center of Richter's net. Niedermayer wound up and slapped the puck hard toward Richter. It went through Richter's legs. Score! The Devils led, 2-0!

The crowd was deafening, and the rock music volume went up a notch or two during the celebration. Messier's words had a hollow ring now when the Rangers went to the locker room trailing, 2-0, after the first period.

The Devils continued to press the Rangers' net during the second period. It appeared that New York coach Mike Keenan was very angry. He called

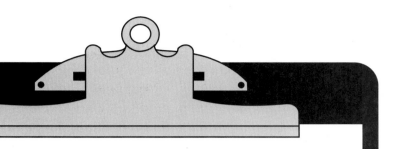

# STATS

Mark Messier seems to be at his best when the games are most important. After the 1996–97 season he ranked second all-time in all three of the major scoring categories for the postseason.

## Playoff Points

| Player | Goals | Assists | Points |
|---|---|---|---|
| 1. Wayne Gretzky | 122 | 260 | 382 |
| 2. **Mark Messier** | **109** | **186** | **295** |
| 3. Jari Kurri | 106 | 127 | 233 |
| 4. Glenn Anderson | 93 | 121 | 214 |
| 5. Paul Coffey | 59 | 136 | 195 |

## Playoff Goals

| Player | Goals |
|---|---|
| 1. Wayne Gretzky | 122 |
| 2. **Mark Messier** | **109** |
| 3. Jari Kurri | 106 |
| 4. Glenn Anderson | 93 |
| 5. Mike Bossy | 85 |

## Playoff Assists

| Player | Assists |
|---|---|
| 1. Wayne Gretzky | 260 |
| 2. **Mark Messier** | **186** |
| 3. Paul Coffey | 136 |
| 4. Jari Kurri | 127 |
| 5. Glenn Anderson | 121 |

a time-out. Usually coaches will say some words to their players during this thirty-second break, but Keenan said nothing. He just stared at his players. The Rangers responded. They started to check more and to defend Richter better.

The score remained 2-0 until the final two minutes of the second period. Messier picked up the puck and skated as hard as he could toward the Devils defensive zone. As Messier moved across the Devils' blue line, he skillfully dropped the puck gently for Rangers forward Alexei Kovalev, who was about thirty-five feet to the right of Brodeur. Kovalev faked his first shot. He then moved in ten more feet. Kovalev wound up and slapped the puck toward Brodeur. The Devils' goalie stretched out his left leg. Too late! Score! The Rangers fans roared.

New York now trailed only 2-1 after two periods. They still had twenty more minutes of play to take the lead. If the Rangers did not score in the third period, their season would be over. The pressure was squarely on Messier's shoulders. He was the captain. He had already helped the Edmonton Oilers to five Stanley Cups. His teammates looked to him for leadership and scoring.

Messier started the third period flying. He flew past the Devils' defense and skated around the net. As he was about to put the puck past Brodeur, the net was dislodged, and it was ruled no goal by Fraser. There seemed to be a fire in Messier's eyes as he got ready for the face-off. The season was on the line. He would have to take charge if the Rangers were to have any chance of beating the Devils.

Leetch picked up the puck not too far from Richter and started skating. He then passed it to Kovalev, who skated over the Devils' blue line and pushed the puck forward to Messier. Now Messier was at a tough angle, since he didn't directly face the net. Most of his weight was on his right side, and he shot left-handed. So if he shot the puck, it was going to be a hard shot to score on. Messier gathered the puck on his stick and glanced quickly at Brodeur. Messier was about twenty feet to the right of Brodeur. Messier shot the puck and kept it on the ice, hoping he would beat Brodeur's left leg to the puck. Score! Messier's goal tied the score at 2-2 just 2:48 into the third period.

The Rangers' faithful were now roaring. They were outnumbered by the Devils fans but were not being outshouted. The Rangers fans sensed something special was happening. Kovalev picked up the puck near the center ice line and slipped a pass to Leetch. The Rangers defenseman, known for his offensive skills, skated across the Devils' blue line to the left of Brodeur.

**FACT**

Mark Messier was the only Ranger with a $150,000 Madison Square Garden sky box in his contract.

As Leetch skated by, he slid the puck back to Kovalev, who blasted the puck in one motion toward Brodeur. The goalie kicked out his left leg and deflected the puck in the air. The puck bounced down to the ice, toward a group of players. Trailing the play was Messier, but he skated quickly toward the bouncing puck. Messier, who was holding his stick on the ice as he had been taught to do when he was young, swatted at the puck. The shot skipped past Brodeur's left leg and into the net. Goal!

The Rangers fans roared as if they were at a home game. Messier exulted and flashed a big smile. His goal with 7:48 left in the third period gave New York its first lead of the game, at 3-2. But Messier quickly put his game face back on. It was not going to be easy to defend against the Devils' scoring. New Jersey was one of the best teams in the league. In fact, the Devils were to win the Stanley Cup in 1995. But this was Messier's year.

The Devils started to press and put pressure on Richter and the Rangers. Richter continued to make great saves, and the minutes started to tick away . . . six minutes left . . . five minutes left . . . four minutes left . . . three minutes left . . . but with 2:49 remaining, New York forward Glenn Anderson was called for a penalty by Fraser. New Jersey would now have

*Messier swats the puck past Devils' goalie Martin Brodeur and into the net. This goal gave the Rangers a 3-2 lead in Game 6.*

a one-man advantage for the next two minutes. The Devils fans started to become louder. The Rangers were able to melt the clock down to 1:53 left without a Devils goal. A face-off occurred to the right of Richter. Messier, known for being a great face-off man, was ready to take it.

The Devils, deciding that they had nothing to lose, took Brodeur out of the net and put another skater on to add more offense. In doing so, they would leave the net open without a goalie. It was a risky move, but having another skater would give New Jersey a two-man advantage instead of just one.

Messier took the face-off deep in the Rangers zone. He pushed the puck back to defenseman Doug Lidster. But Lidster made a big mistake. He did not pass the puck with enough speed. Devils forward John McClain intercepted the pass behind the Rangers' net. He quickly spotted a Devil racing toward the net and passed the puck to the left of Richter. Messier, sensing Lidster's trouble, moved quickly to the front of Richter. Messier intercepted the pass, and he never hesitated. He quickly slapped the puck toward the Devils' goal. It was about a hundred feet away, but he was confident he could score. Goal! The puck went right into the center of the net, for a 4-2 Rangers lead.

Messier was mobbed by his teammates at the bench. He had scored his fourth Stanley Cup hat trick, his first as a member of the Rangers. Even more important, his heroic efforts in the third period enabled the Rangers to survive and play again in the seventh game. Messier's drive to win another Stanley Cup was only beginning.

# Chapter 2

# The Young Star

For as long as he could remember, Mark Messier had dreamed of becoming a great hockey player and winning the Stanley Cup. He would picture himself holding the Cup high over his head while the fans cheered and his family watched. After all, if it weren't for his family, Mark might never have picked up a hockey stick.

His grandfather, Jack Dea, was a goaltender for the Edmonton Eskimos. Then there was Great-uncle Murray Murdoch, who once was captain of the New York Rangers. Uncle Murray used to spend hours telling little Mark stories about how he had played for the Rangers. Neither knew that one day Mark would grow up to be a Rangers captain, too.

And then there was Mark's father, Doug. He was

a defenseman in the Western Hockey Association. Doug was a tough player who earned the nickname Magilla Gorilla. He never lifted weights during his playing days, but in the off-season he worked loading cement trucks. "Each bag weighed 87½ pounds," he remembered, "and it was sort of a competition to load the truck three bags at a time."[1]

Mark Messier joined his hockey family on January 18, 1961, in Edmonton, Alberta, Canada. He and his three siblings—Paul, Mary Kay, and Jennifer—spent their early years in Portland, Oregon. Doug Messier played minor-league hockey there for the Portland Buckaroos. Mark and his older brother would spend hours shooting pucks in the carport of their family home. "I took to it naturally," said Messier. "I got a lot of hockey knowledge watching my Dad play, and being around hockey all my life helped. He knew what it took for me to play pro. Not that he pushed me. He more or less let me make my own decisions about playing hockey. When I made that decision, he helped me out tremendously."[2]

Mark was indeed very determined to play hockey. He would go and watch his father practice every day. One morning, Doug wanted to go to practice by himself. He got up early and tried to sneak out of the house. But there was eight-year-old Mark standing

*Mark Messier enjoyed the limelight that comes with playing professional sports in New York City.*

in the driveway, blocking the car. He stubbornly refused to move until his father promised to take him, too!

His mother, Mary Jean Messier, remembered another time when her son was very determined. "There was this ornery black Shetland pony that Mark named Billy," she recalled. "The man next to us got rid of Billy because he used to bite everybody. He gave him to us. No one could ever do anything with that horse. Except Mark."[3]

The Messiers always taught their children to be team players. Mark was very close to his brother and sisters. They would always stick together and support each other. When they were at the playground, they would challenge the other children in games of touch football. "Most brothers wouldn't choose their sisters for a team," said Mary Kay. "Not us. It was always the family, together."[4]

Mark's father stopped playing hockey in 1970 and moved his family back to Edmonton, in the Canadian province of Alberta. He then became a coach for the Spruce Grove Mets, who won the Canadian Tier Two Junior "A" Championship Centennial Cup in 1975. One year later, he coached both Mark and Paul on a Tier Two Junior Team. Mark was fifteen then. He only weighed 155 pounds, but he was a very good skater. Paul was the star of the team. He was a great puck handler and scorer, and was much better than Mark. "I still hadn't grown," Messier said. "I wasn't sure I could make the team, so I worked like crazy all summer."[5] He did make the team, but continued to struggle. One night, Mark found his father's team roster. There was his name: Mark Messier. Next to it there were three big question marks. "It really scared me," said Messier. "I thought I might get cut."[6] For the next two seasons, Mark worked really hard. He put on more weight and became a promising player with a determination to win.

Of the two brothers, it seemed that Paul would be the one to make it to the NHL. "Paul couldn't skate like Mark," said their mother. "But as far as scoring, he had softer hands."[7] Everyone on the team, including Mark, looked up to Paul for scoring and leadership. But in the end, it would be Mark who made it to the big leagues. Paul went on to play four seasons in the minor leagues in North America. He only made it up to the NHL for nine games with the Colorado Rockies. Then he played seven pro seasons in Germany. But he still remained one of his little brother's biggest supporters and advisors. When Mark finally became a New York Ranger, Doug and Paul negotiated his contract.

Messier became especially close to Mary Kay as

**FACT**

Messier loves to have fun. When he first joined the Rangers as their new captain, he organized group activities—parties, barbecues, golf events, even a team trip to the Paramount movie studios. At masquerade parties, he liked to dress up as Tarzan or the Joker.

they grew older. One of his best childhood friends, Darrell Morrow, married Mary Kay. Messier was the best man, and he spent two weeks in Hawaii helping his sister get ready for the big event.

Messier, his parents, and Mary Kay also ran a clothing company. They named it Number Eleven, since that's the number Messier has always worn. He even helped his family by modeling the clothes for ads. Unfortunately, the business ran into trouble and was forced to close. It was a difficult time for the Messier family, but they always supported each other.

When Messier finally left Canada and moved to New York to join the Rangers, his family moved with him. Mary Kay and Paul formed Messier Management International. Together they handle Mark Messier's product endorsements. Messier's father, Doug, is his agent, and negotiates his contracts. Hockey may be a big part of Mark Messier's life, but his family plays an even bigger part. If they hadn't been so supportive of his goals, Mark might not have taken a big step when he was only seventeen.

In 1978, just a few months shy of graduating high school, Mark Messier felt it was time to take a risk. He decided to try out for the Indianapolis Racers of the World Hockey Association. The WHA

*When they were growing up, Messier's younger brother Paul received more attention for his hockey skills. Today Mark Messier is one of the most well-known hockey players in the world.*

was a league trying to compete with the National Hockey League. The WHA was able to persuade some superstars from the NHL for more money. Though the WHA was not a better league than the NHL, Messier was still going up against some very skilled hockey players. He was also going up against people who had much more hockey experience than he did. Most of the players in the WHA were ten years older than Mark.

Despite these disadvantages, Messier was impressive enough during a five-game trial with the Racers to stay in the WHA. He was traded to the Cincinnati Stingers during the 1978–79 season. The challenges started to pile up for him, though. It was not a successful season; in fact, it was very humbling. Messier was only able to score one goal, a lucky shot that came from center ice. Rarely does a professional goalie allow a shot to go in the net from that distance.

One goal in forty-seven games was hardly impressive for any player. Messier was deflated by his first season on the professional level. "Maybe I was in a little over my head," he admitted. "But I thought I could play well enough to get by."[8]

Messier was going to learn the hard way. He was going to learn that talent alone is not enough to get by. And he would learn later that his expectations of his game were a lot higher than those of the average player. So "getting by" was never going to be good enough.

But the best was yet to come for Messier. The WHA was disbanded, and some of the teams from the younger league were merged with the NHL. Messier, who had impressed the Edmonton Oilers' general manager and coach, Glen Sather, in a junior game two years earlier, was chosen in the third round of the 1979 entry draft. Sather was quite pleased that he was able to get Messier. "I had seen him play as a junior, and he had been a leader," Sather said. "Coming off what he did in Cincinnati, he was no sure thing. We were gambling on young players anyway. So we drafted him. When he made the team it was by design, not accident. We wanted players we could teach the game to."[9]

True, Messier was no sure thing for any NHL team, and it was a gamble for Sather to select him. To make things worse, Messier got off to a shaky start. He showed he had confidence and could be aggressive on the ice, but many felt that he was too confident for a teenager playing the NHL. Some perceived Messier's attitude as offensive.

To make matters even worse, Messier showed up to practice late on a couple of occasions, angering Sather. Not only was he tardy for practice; he missed a team flight. Sather had had enough. He needed to punish Messier for these disruptions. "He wasn't dedicated to the game," Sather said. "He had a man's body but a kid's maturity. He had a lot of learning to do."[10]

But Sather made sure that Messier was going to do his learning somewhere else. For his punishment, Messier spent time learning in the minor leagues. Sather felt that Messier needed a touch of humility. He was happy that Messier was confident and aggressive on the ice, but discipline is a major part of any professional athlete's life.

Messier played for the Houston Apollos in the Central Hockey League during the 1979–80 season. In his four games, he showed glimpses of what he could do on a full-time basis. He set up teammates three times with beautiful passes for goals. Sather was very impressed. He didn't waste any more time in recalling Messier back to the NHL.

But it wasn't going to be as easy in the NHL as it was in the minors. Messier was still only nineteen years old. He had only played a couple of years in the juniors. The goalies in the NHL were much bigger, stronger, and more experienced than he was. In seventy-five games with the Oilers, he scored just 12 goals in his rookie year. He also had 21 assists for 33 points. Messier's aggressive style of play also landed him in the penalty box too often, with 133 penalty minutes. He did score his first playoff goal with a goal against Philadelphia. The Oilers, however, were eliminated from the playoffs early.

It was a season of growing pains for both Messier and the Oilers. With the disappointing rookie season in the NHL behind him, he worked very hard during the summer to build up his physical strength and his mental toughness. He was no longer a teenager, and more was going to be expected of him for the 1980–81 season than had been expected last season.

For some reason, though, Messier struggled again at the start of the season. By the end of January, he had only registered 25 points. He was disappointed in himself but still very confident in his ability. Coach Glen Sather was looking for ways to help Messier improve his game. Sather's confidence in Messier was still high. He believed that Messier was someday going to be one of the best players in the NHL. Messier, of course, had always believed that.

Confidence usually rewards athletes who work hard. It did pay off for Sather and Messier, who exploded offensively over the last two months of the regular season, piling up 38 points. Messier had reverted to his aggressive style on the ice, which elevated his confidence even more. His success over the past two months gave the rest of the NHL a glimpse of what was to come for many years.

Messier's stick handling and shooting skills seemed to improve dramatically over the last two months. He almost doubled his offensive production from the previous year. He scored 23 goals and had 40 assists for 63 points. He also cut down on his penalty minutes, which helped him and his team. Sather wanted Messier on the ice as much as possible. "I went straight from Tier Two hockey to the pros and it took a long time for me to adjust," Messier said. "By 1981–82, I was feeling a lot more comfortable. I always thought I had the ability to play. It was just going to take time."[11]

It was his own hard work and the suggestions by Sather that helped Messier move into the top bracket of players in the NHL. Messier had always dreamed of being an All-Star in the NHL. He wanted to achieve much more than the average player, and Sather was going to help him accomplish that. Sather told Messier that he should work on improving his wrist shot and snap shot. It was known around the NHL that Messier had one shot—a slap shot. But all the great players in the NHL had always used several different shots to score past goalies. Messier worked hard during

## FACT

One of Messier's favorite movies is *Caddyshack*. According to his family, he has seen it a hundred times, and often does impersonations of its star, Bill Murray.

training camp to develop those skills. His hard work paid off.

The 1981–82 season was Messier's breakout year. He was named to the NHL All-Star team for the first time. Messier was showing that he could score effectively with three different shots—slap shot, snap shot, and wrist shot. He scored 50 goals for the first time in his career and also added 38 assists for 88 points. The Oilers were now one of the best teams in the NHL. Due to Messier's terrific year and the stellar play of Wayne Gretzky, Edmonton climbed to win its division. It looked as if this was going to be the year of Messier and company. Playoffs are a different season and Messier and the young Oilers learned another lesson: Take nothing for granted. The lowly Los Angeles Kings knocked Edmonton out of the playoffs in the first round.

Sather and Messier were very upset and disappointed. It took a while before Messier was able to overcome his disappointment. He worked even harder during the off-season to get himself in shape for the 1982–83 season. Again, his hard work paid off. He scored 48 goals to go along with his 58 assists for a total of 106 points, the first time he cracked the 100-point plateau.

Messier was even more brilliant in the Stanley Cup playoffs. He threatened the record for most

*Mark Messier gives teammate Wayne Gretzky a high five after Gretzky scored a goal for the Campbell Conference All-Star team. Messier made his first all-star appearance during the 1981–82 season.*

goals in a playoff year. In fifteen games, he scored 15 goals. He also added 6 assists for a total of 21 points. In the Smythe Division finals against the Calgary Flames, he scored 4 goals in one game, proving he was among the best in the NHL. Messier had previously scored 4 goals against the Montreal Canadiens, but that was during the regular season.

Despite the effort by Messier, the Oilers fell short in the Stanley Cup finals against the New York Islanders. The Islanders had won the Cup three straight years with such stars as Denis Potvin, Clark Gillies, Billy Smith, and Bryan Trottier. New York was not about to let the Cup go.

What the Oilers had accomplished during the 1982–83 season was a warning to the Islanders as well as to the rest of the NHL. It was a warning that the Oilers, full of young faces and energetic legs, were ready to try and wrestle the Cup away from a New York team that had won it for four straight years.

**FACT**

When Mark Messier was selected to play in the NHL All-Star Game for the first time in 1982, he wanted to fly his family to Washington, D.C., for the game. His father told him it was too expensive, but Messier insisted, saying there was no point in making the team if he couldn't share it with his family.

# Chapter 3

# Winning the Cup

Throughout the course of Mark Messier's amazing career, he has been asked to perform tasks not normally associated with the average player. Messier has never been one to back away from a challenge whether it comes from a coach, player, or himself. This is what has made Mark Messier great. He usually delivers successful results when called upon.

The 1983–84 season started like the previous two seasons. The Oilers were emerging as a powerhouse in the NHL, while Messier was gaining his reputation as one of hockey's best players. The Oilers and Messier got off to a good start. Messier, playing his usual position of left wing, was scoring goals and helping his teammates score with his beautiful passes. Messier has always made it known that he feels better when he can help a teammate score rather than himself.

Messier's speed along the left wing was one of the most beautiful things to watch during an Oilers game. Nobody was able to match his combination of speed and strength. His puck-handling skills along the left wing were also becoming impossible to match. Coach Glen Sather wanted to give the Oilers four strong lines. Sather thought about the solution for a long time. He weighed the strengths of Messier's game—his speed and muscle—along with his leadership. Sather wanted someone with those characteristics to play center ice for him.

Sather eventually came to the conclusion that there was nobody other than Messier who could handle the added responsibilities. If Messier was moved from left wing to center, he would be counted on more to check the opposing team's top scorer, and he would also be counted on to set up his teammates for more goals. On February 15, 1984, Sather moved Messier to the center ice position. Questions arose as to whether it was wise to move an All-Star left-winger to center ice. After all, just one month earlier, Messier had led the Oilers to an amazing victory over Minnesota. Messier set up teammates six times for goals. His 6 assists were a career high!

The move appeared to strengthen the Oilers. Edmonton had more balance scoring in its lineup, due to Messier's incredible ability to find teammates open for shots and goals. His move to center ice seemed to have solidified the Oilers as true contenders for the Stanley Cup. The Oilers continued to strive toward their goal of winning the Stanley Cup. Messier's goals went down to 37 for the regular season, but he finished with 64 assists for a total of 101 points. Edmonton finished first in the NHL with a 57-18-5 record for 119 points.

Due to the great strides in the regular season, there were high hopes by the Oilers fans that this team could win the Stanley Cup. It was going to be a struggle, because Edmonton would have to try to wrestle the Cup away from the four-time defending champions, the New York Islanders. Many hockey experts thought before the season that both teams would meet again in the Finals—and they were right!

The Islanders were trying to claim their fifth straight Stanley Cup. They had grown accustomed to winning the Cup, and they had such superstars as right-winger Mike Bossy, Bobby Nystrom, and Butch Goring. The Oilers, though, had revenge on their minds. They had been beaten badly the previous year in the Finals.

**FACT**

Mark Messier wants to play hockey until the year 2000, when he will reach the age of forty. If he does that, he will have played in four decades.

"But we're also a lot better in our end with the puck," said Oilers scout Barry Fraser. "And by putting Mark [Messier] at center, we have two very physical center icemen where we really had nobody before. Our defense has been criticized for three years, and that's never been a problem. . . .

"Maybe the difference there is that, this year," Fraser added, "nothing less than the Stanley Cup was going to be good enough for these guys."[1]

There was no doubt that it wasn't going to be good enough for Messier unless the Oilers won the Stanley Cup. The dream of winning the Stanley Cup was something that he had worked so hard for all his life. A crowd of 17,502 packed the Northlands Coliseum in Edmonton to greet the Oilers, who returned home with a 3-1 advantage over the Islanders. It was an advantage that many hockey experts did not think could have existed, because of the New Yorkers' experience. One more win for the Oilers, and Edmonton would win its first Stanley Cup!

On May 19, 1984, Edmonton was facing Billy Smith, one of the best playoff goalies in history. He had been the man in the nets for the previous four Stanley Cup victories by the Islanders. But the Oilers just had too much firepower for Smith. When Messier wasn't peppering the New York net with

*Warding off Larry Playfair of the Los Angeles Kings, Mark Messier maintains possession. Besides being a dangerous scorer, Messier was also known as one of the most physical centermen in the league.*

offensive moves, Wayne Gretzky was. Gretzky was able to gain the puck at center ice and move in on Smith all alone. Gretzky faked a shot and then slipped it past Smith, for an Edmonton 1-0 lead. Gretzky would add another goal off a three-on-one break to give the Oilers a 2-0 advantage.

The Oilers crowd was roaring; this could be a very special night. Smith was replaced in goal by Rollie Melanson after just one period. The Oilers didn't care who was in the nets. They had just one direction—straight toward the New York net. Ken Linseman and Jari Kurri each scored a goal early in the second period, to give Edmonton a 4-0 lead. Linseman's and Kurri's scores came when New York was one man short due to penalties.

The Islanders struck back with two quick goals at the start of the third period. Messier, though, was not about to let the Oilers let the Cup slip away. "I've been rehearsing the moment for the last two months, maybe the last five years," he said. "Every night before I went to bed I went over what I'd do, how it would feel [to carry the Cup]. I've been dreaming about skating around with it since I was six years old, really. Watching the Islanders with the Cup last year hurt the most."[2]

There wasn't going to be any hurt this year for Messier and the Oilers. An empty net goal late in the third period gave Edmonton a 5-2 lead. The Islanders decided to put Melanson on the bench and put another skater on the ice for more offense. It did not work.

Just seconds remained when Messier realized his dream was coming true. A grin flashed across his face from ear to ear as he gazed into a crowd of jubilant faces and heard the roaring fans. He was going to get a chance to carry the Stanley Cup around the Northlands Coliseum.

"If we didn't win this team wouldn't be together ever again," Messier said. "If we did win . . . well then we could stay together for a really long time. If we have a team identity it's our camaraderie. I've never seen 20 or 25 guys that get along so well."[3]

Messier was also honored for his individual achievements during the Stanley Cup playoffs. He scored 8 goals and added 18 assists for a total of 26 points. Gretzky scored more total points, but Messier's leadership and defensive work against the Islanders' superstar center, Bryan Trottier, earned him the Conn Smythe Trophy—given to the playoff's most valuable player.

Islanders star defenseman Denis Potvin commented, "I felt no shame turning the Cup over to them I'm damn proud . . . several Oilers talked about idolizing us as we shook hands. One great

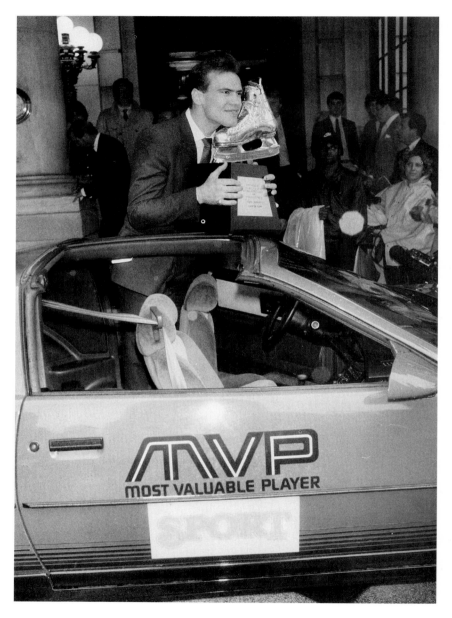

*After the 1983–84 season, Mark Messier was awarded the Conn Smythe Trophy for his role in leading the Edmonton Oilers to their first Stanley Cup championship. He is shown here with his awards—a trophy and a new car.*

team turning it over to a team that was great all year. They deserved it."[4]

Now it was time for everyone to praise and idolize the Oilers. There was a celebration and a parade in Edmonton. Messier and company were the toast of the town. Though they were very happy that they claimed the Stanley Cup, they were more interested in forming a dynasty. Along with structuring a dynasty, though, come injuries and pain.

During the 1984–85 season, in the February 4 game against the Winnipeg Jets, Messier felt some pain in his left knee. He was forced to sit out and mend his aching left knee. The Oilers lost the services of one of their best players for fifteen games.

Messier played just fifty-five games and saw his offensive production slip. He scored 23 goals and had 31 assists for 54 points. But now the playoffs—a new season to build upon—were here, and Messier was ready. He scored 12 goals and had 13 assists for 25 points in just eighteen playoff games.

Edmonton fought its way into the Stanley Cup Finals again. There was a new opponent, a Philadelphia Flyers team that was the youngest in the league. Suddenly the Oilers were no longer the upstarts, but they now had experience on their side. This propelled them to a 3-1 advantage over the Flyers. Messier's effort helped Edmonton to within

The Edmonton Oilers defeated the Chicago Blackhawks to win the 1985 Campbell Conference Finals. They would then go on to face the Philadelphia Flyers, and try to repeat as Stanley Cup champions.

one game of winning their second straight Stanley Cup.

Game 5 was played in Edmonton. It looked like a certain Oilers victory, and it was. Defenseman Paul Coffey scored 2 goals in the first three minutes of the game to give the Oilers an immediate 2-0 lead. Philadelphia eventually changed its goalie to Bob Froese. Bringing in a goalie who is not warmed up is a mistake, but Philadelphia really didn't have a choice, since its starting goalie, Pelle Lindbergh, had a sore knee.

There was no sympathy from Messier. He had a job to do. He scored quickly on Froese and added another goal, to give Edmonton a commanding 8-3 lead. There was going to be another Stanley Cup celebration for Edmonton fans. The Oilers' second straight Stanley Cup victory raised eyebrows around the NHL. Could these Oilers be a dynasty? Many thought the Oilers wouldn't be able to repeat. Now many were wondering if Edmonton might be able to win three straight Cups.

Pain continued to follow Messier around during the next regular season. In the 1985–86 campaign, he suffered a hairline fracture of his left foot and missed seventeen games because of the injury. He came back to the Oilers on January 11, when Edmonton played Montreal. It appeared that his left foot was fine. Mark was motoring around with his usual speed and aggressiveness. Two nights later, the Oilers saw what they had been missing for seventeen games. Messier assisted on 2 goals and later scored the game-winning goal against the Boston Bruins.

Despite playing in just sixty-three games, Messier totaled 84 points on 35 goals and 49 assists. As a team, the Oilers weren't as good. Edmonton had a good regular season, but it was eliminated from the playoffs early on. Any dreams of a dynasty had evaporated. Messier went home sad but started his training.

Messier had had to overcome early season injuries during two previous seasons. He wanted to avoid that at all costs. He was also driven to make the 1986–87 season his best. He did, and he was simply brilliant. He returned to the same high-flying aggressive style of skating and play that had been missing a little during the previous year. He was healthy this time, and it showed in his play.

In seventy-seven games, Messier scored 37 goals and had a career high of 70 assists for 107 points. He was determined to bring the Stanley Cup back to Edmonton. The Oilers' opponents in the Finals were the Flyers again. Two seasons ago, Philadelphia had lost to Edmonton in the Finals, but this Flyer team was much more experienced. It showed.

Whenever the Oilers jumped out to a lead, the Flyers quickly counterattacked. The Oilers, showing their mastery around the net, did claim a 3-1 advantage. Many thought Philadelphia was dead, but the Flyers won Games 5 and 6, tying the series. Very few teams have ever come back from that far down in a series. This made the Oilers' fans very uncomfortable and nervous. Could the Oilers lose the series after being so far ahead?

Game 7 was played in Edmonton. This was an advantage for the Oilers, but the Flyers had the momentum going into the game. Edmonton fans became more nervous when Messier was called for a penalty just thirty-four seconds into the game. To make matters even worse for the Oilers, their best defenseman, Paul Coffey, was also called for a penalty, giving Philadelphia a two-man advantage.

This advantage by the Flyers was too much for even the Oilers to overcome. Flyers winger Murray Craven was able to shoot the puck past Edmonton goalie Grant Fuhr. The score came after only 1:41 had elapsed in the game. Oilers fans were silent and stunned. It looked as if Philadelphia might win.

Messier wasn't going to let the Oilers fade away so easily, though. He started talking to his linemates,

## FACT

In the 1987 documentary *The Boys on the Bus*, Mark Messier and Wayne Gretzky discussed why they are playing hockey. Gretzky said he plays for the fun of it. Messier said he plays to challenge himself.

encouraging them to start attacking. His linemates, Kent Nilsson and Glenn Anderson, responded. Messier, Anderson, and Nilsson moved past the tough Philadelphia checking forwards and to the blue line. Anderson moved around a Flyers defenseman and passed to Nilsson. He saw Messier streaking toward the Flyers goal and put the puck on Messier's stick. In one motion, Messier peeked at the net, spotted an opening, and whacked the puck toward Flyers goalie Ron Hextall. The Oilers crowd roared. Their leader had scored and tied the game at 1-1.

Messier and his linemates continued to assault the Flyers' goal, but Hextall, who eventually would be named the MVP of the playoffs, was equally brilliant. In the second period, Jari Kurri scored for the Oilers, to give them a 2-1 lead. It stayed that way until the last three minutes of the third period. Anderson scored at 17:36 to put the Flyers away.

The celebration began. Messier and the Oilers had reclaimed the Stanley Cup! As the seconds ticked away, Mark danced a jig around the ice and tossed his gloves into the stands to some lucky fans. The roar seemed louder than it was in previous years. Maybe this was because the fans saw that winning the Cup isn't so easy, though the Oilers seemed to make it look that way. They cheered Messier the loudest.

"Messier was unbelievable," Philadelphia winger Rick Tocchet said. "He was a force. He won it for them tonight."[5]

Messier's drive helped erase summer-long doubts about whether the Oilers would ever be able to recapture the Stanley Cup. "The way they played tonight they showed they are the world's best team," Flyers coach Mike Keenan said.[6]

The Oilers had one of the world's best players in Mark Messier. But as the Oilers were celebrating with a parade and party in Edmonton, the question arose again: Could the Oilers repeat as Stanley Cup champions in the 1987–88 season?

# Chapter 4

# The Captain

**T**here wasn't much rest for Mark Messier during the summer of 1987. Messier was called upon by his country to represent Canada in an international competition called the Canada Cup. During this tournament, some of the world's best hockey teams are invited to play at various sites in the United States and Canada. The Canada Cup has a format similar to that of the Olympics. Since Messier was born in Edmonton, he was more than happy to play for the Canadian team. He had also played for the 1984 team, and his leadership enabled Canada to win the Canada Cup in 1984 and 1987. Canada had a dramatic come-from-behind victory to beat the Soviet team, 6-5, to win the 1987 Cup in the third game.

This was a good tuneup for Messier for the 1987–88 season. He was looking forward to defending the Stanley Cup. Messier reached some eye-popping milestones during the regular season. He equaled his production in goals from the previous season with 37 and added 74 assists for 111 points. He also led the Oilers with 7 game-winning goals. This was no surprise, since many regarded him as one of the best players in the game when the outcome was on the line.

Messier also compiled 4 points in five different games, showing how explosive his offensive skills were. In thirty-three games, he had 2 or more points. Messier was a model of consistency. He scored his 300th NHL career goal on March 15 against Buffalo and scored a point in each of fourteen consecutive games from October 31 to November 29.

Edmonton eagerly awaited the arrival of the playoffs. They were now certainly used to playing for the Stanley Cup, while other teams seemed to be uptight and nervous. This was no problem for the Oilers, though. Messier and company made their way into the Stanley Cup Finals again, but a different opponent awaited the Oilers—the Boston Bruins. The Bruins featured one of the best young players in the game in defenseman Ray Bourque. Many longtime Bruins fans compared Bourque to former Boston star and hockey legend Bobby Orr. It certainly was unfair to compare Bourque to Orr, but Bourque was a great defenseman. The Oilers were the NHL's best overall team. They had shown this during the first three rounds of the playoffs. The Oilers had only lost two of the fourteen playoff games.

Edmonton's domination showed in the first three games of the final series. The Oilers commandeered a 3-0 advantage and seemed poised to carry the Cup away again. There was a crowd of over fourteen thousand people at the Boston Garden for Game 4 on May 26, 1988. The Oilers just had to play sixty more minutes of good hockey, and it was likely they would win. Surely then, people would think of Edmonton as one of hockey's greatest dynasties.

"I think it's fair to say this team is better than last year's though, or that our first Stanley Cup team that beat the Islanders was number one," said Oilers coach Glen Sather. "Every team has its own characters and own people that make things different. Each team had its own personality. They've all been great. And all been winners."[1]

All of the Oilers' Stanley Cup winners have had Mark Messier on their team. Messier followed up his great regular season play with an even more

*Knocking people out of his way, Mark Messier skates over one of the Boston Bruins. Boston was Edmonton's opponent in the 1988 Stanley Cup Finals.*

brilliant playoff showing. During fourteen straight playoff games, Messier had a point or more in each one. During that streak, there were four games in which he scored 4 points. His 11 goals and 23 assists for 34 points made him second in the NHL. It was to nobody's surprise that because of Messier's play, Edmonton claimed the Cup. Edmonton's 6-3 win on Bruin ice gave the Oilers a surprising sweep.

Oiler fans didn't have the whole summer to celebrate winning the Cup. The unthinkable happened: Edmonton traded hockey legend and superstar Wayne Gretzky, the Oilers' goal-scoring machine and captain, to the Los Angeles Kings in August 1988. Gretzky had wanted more money and wanted to be close to Los Angeles so his wife, Janet Jones, who desired to be an actress, would have ample opportunity to work there.

Now the Oilers were going to have to rely even more on Messier's leadership and skills. He felt he could handle the pressure, but it proved to be a burden at first. "The measure of Mark's game is not in goals and assists," Gretzky said. "The statistic he cares about is the number of Stanley Cups won."[2]

The Oilers were now solely Messier's team. He was named team captain after Gretzky was traded, and he scored 33 goals and added 61 assists for 94 points. But the Oilers did not have the same drive and motivation they had possessed last season. They ran out of gas in the playoffs. Messier led the Oilers in playoff scoring with 12 points, but his team did not follow his actions. "It all rested on his shoulders for the first time in his life," said defenseman Kevin Lowe. "Mark will disagree with me, but I think he tried to do too much. Instead of being a power forward, he tried to be everything. At times, he tried too much to be a playmaker."[3]

Messier was extremely disappointed with the results of the 1988–89 season. He took a lot of the blame on his own shoulders. This made him even more determined to make the 1989–90 season his best ever. Critics thought he would never be able to score as much now because Gretzky was gone, but Messier was great from the start of the regular season. He played in a career-high seventy-nine games. In sixty-four of those games, he scored at least one point.

Messier consistently showed brilliance. On November 21, he made some terrific stick-handling moves to score 3 goals against Vancouver, to help the Oilers win, 4-3. People around the NHL noticed the difference in Mark Messier from the previous season. "Messier was the story," said Vancouver coach Bob McCammon. "When he's going, he's a force. He's a guy you've got to take physically, and we didn't do it. We never laid a glove on him. But that's why he's so great. Mark can be pretty scary to watch out there."[4]

For most of the season, it was very scary to the rest of the NHL to see a glaring Messier motoring down the center of the ice. For Oilers fans, he was a pretty sight of speed and grace all season.

Messier scored 45 goals and added a career-high 84 assists for a career-high 129 points, an answer to critics who claimed that the Oilers couldn't get along without Gretzky. But the regular season was just the first challenge for Messier and the Oilers. They were determined to prove to the hockey world that they could claim the Cup without Gretzky.

"We all got together in a room to watch the Super Bowl," said Messier. "The San Francisco 49ers won the championship and we saw what kind of dedication it took to win a championship. It opened a lot of eyes on our hockey club. We were missing Wayne [Gretzky] and we said, 'Let's go and show him how much we miss him by winning. He knows how we feel now, he's with us.'"[5]

Messier was also brilliant in the playoffs. He had

eight multiple-point games and tied for the lead in playoff scoring with 31 points. His offensive production and leadership guided the Oilers into the Stanley Cup Finals against a familiar opponent—the Boston Bruins. This Bruins team was vastly improved and had gained some more playoff experience since the teams had met two years ago, but the Oilers would not give the Bruins any satisfaction. The Bruins weren't swept as they were the last time, but it was close.

Boston's 2-1 victory in Game 3 was its only victory so far in the first four games. Game 5 was held before 14,448 fans at the Boston Garden. The Bruins weren't going to die easily. They matched the Oilers with body check to body check and shot for shot. The Bruins and the Oilers each put 10 shots on net, but neither team scored in the first period.

Edmonton broke loose in the second period. Glenn Anderson picked up the puck in his own end and wiggled and weaved around several Bruins as he broke in on former teammate Andy Moog. Anderson faked and shot. Goal! The Oilers led, 1-0, 1:17 into the second period. Craig Simpson added a goal just eight minutes later, and deflated the Boston crowd. Simpson's score gave the Oilers a comfortable 2-0 lead after two periods.

## FACT

Gordie Howe became the first hockey player to reach 1,000 points when he did it in 1960 as a member of the Detroit Red Wings. Thirty-one years later, Mark Messier reached the same milestone on January 13, 1991.

During the intermission, Messier told the Oilers to continue to attack the net. The Oilers listened. Messier's assist set up Steve Smith's score seven minutes into the third period. This appeared to have doomed the Bruins. Three goals were an awful lot to score against the Oilers. To make matters worse for the Bruins, Joe Murphy of the Oilers tallied the fourth goal, sealing the Edmonton win. The Bruins did score a goal, but it was too late. Time had almost ticked away the final seconds.

This was Messier's team. All eyes from the Oilers looked to him for the leadership, and he knew it. The last second peeled off the clock on May 24, 1990, and the critics were silenced forever. Yes, the Oilers could win without Wayne Gretzky. The Oilers still had Mark Messier.

A massive celebration erupted on the ice before the silent Boston fans. Many Bruins fans had felt they had a better chance to win the Stanley Cup this year because of the absence of Gretzky, but they seemed to forget about Messier. Now they watched the Oilers' captain carry hockey's most prized possession around their ancient arena. "It's like trying to wrestle an alligator," said Bruins forward Bobby Carpenter, describing trying to check Messier. "He's strong and slippery, but, most of all, he's very dangerous."[6]

*Overcome with emotion, Mark Messier hoists the Stanley Cup over his head. With the departure of Wayne Gretzky, Messier was selected as captain of the Edmonton Oilers, and in 1990 led them to another championship.*

He was dangerous to his opponents, but such a joy to watch for the Oilers and their fans. Messier's dangerous skills during the regular season were rewarded. He received hockey's most prized individual award. The sportswriters named him the league's most valuable player by awarding him the Hart Trophy. Wayne who?! "Wayne was a little more visible," said Lowe. "But for as long as I can remember, Mark has been a leader on this hockey team, if not the leader."[7]

For the first time, Messier was receiving the recognition that he truly deserved. He has never reached for such recognition, since his only goal has been to win the Stanley Cup. "There's always some point in life when a player is going to have the best year of his career," said Oilers coach John Muckler, who took over for Glen Sather. "Maybe this is the one for Mark."[8]

There was very little rest for Messier. He was again a member of Team Canada in the Canada Cup, and he helped the Canadians keep the Cup. But Messier wasn't totally happy. He had seen Gretzky move on and be paid well in Los Angeles. Since Messier was among the best players in the world, he wanted to be compensated fairly for his efforts, which helped Edmonton make a lot of money. But he was still under contract, and he had an obligation to play for the Oilers until something was resolved.

Messier was ready to start the 1990–91 season, but on October 16, he injured his left knee. He missed nineteen games due to the injury. Just when he was getting in the groove, more pain followed. He fractured his left thumb on February 18 and missed another eight games. When he was not in the lineup, the Oilers were 8-17-2. In the first ten games Messier was out, the Oilers lost nine straight games! When Messier was in the lineup, Edmonton was 29-20-4. It was apparent that the Oilers had trouble winning without their captain.

This was not going to be Messier's year, because of the injuries, and it certainly wasn't Edmonton's year either. The Oilers bowed out during the playoffs, and Messier went home disappointed and frustrated—because of his injury-filled year, and because he had not straightened out his contract problem.

The Oilers settled the dispute on October 4, 1991, just before the 1991–92 season began. Then the unthinkable happened again. Just when Oilers fans were getting over Gretzky's departure by celebrating Messier's performance and Stanley Cup victory, Edmonton traded Messier to the New York Rangers. This produced anger and shock in Edmonton, but it caused joy and celebration in New York.

## FACT

The 1989–90 season was truly a memorable one for Mark Messier. Not only did the Oilers win the Stanley Cup, but he had a career-best record of 45 goals and 84 assists. He won the Hart Trophy as the NHL's Most Valuable Player, and the Lester B. Pearson Award, which was given to him by his fellow players.

The Rangers hadn't won a Stanley Cup since 1940, but this was going to change, according to the Rangers fans. Messier was coming, Messier the Messiah! Could the long Stanley Cup drought be over for New York Rangers fans? Another challenge awaited Mark Messier in the sports capital of the world.

*Mark Messier and former teammate Paul Coffey fight for the puck in the 1991 NHL All-Star game. Due to financial troubles Edmonton's championship teams were being broken up. In October of 1991, Messier was dealt to the New York Rangers.*

# Chapter 5

# Leading the Rangers

**N**ineteen forty! Nineteen forty! The Nassau Coliseum crowd shouted this whenever the Rangers and the Islanders played on Long Island. The year 1940 symbolized failure to the New York Rangers. It was the last year the Rangers won the Stanley Cup. But Rangers fans felt that fate would be kinder to them now that New York had Mark Messier on the team. After all, Messier was a proven winner. He had played for five Edmonton teams that won the Cup.

"Winning is not about where you're playing," Messier said, "but what's in your heart. I feel I can still do it. I have a lot of great hockey in me . . . in order to get there again."[1]

There was no doubt that Messier had a lot of great hockey left in him. His biggest challenge was to lead a

**FACT**

On October 7, 1991, Mark Messier was announced as the new captain of the Rangers at their first home game. Many of the former captains were there. Messier skated down the line, shaking their hands. Who was last on line? Murray Murdoch, eighty-eight, the oldest living Ranger—and Messier's great-uncle!

franchise that many people scoffed at and considered perhaps the most underachieving hockey team in history. Individually, Messier proved he was worth the trade the Rangers had made. He scored 35 goals and had 72 assists for 107 points in 1991–92. He fell just two points short of tying a Rangers record during the regular season. His regular season accomplishments were recognized; he was named the NHL's MVP.

Individual awards and regular season accomplishments are not what Mark Messier is about. The Rangers traded for him to have him perform his heroics in the playoffs. The Rangers did win an exciting first-round matchup with the rival New Jersey Devils, 4-3. But their next opponents were the Pittsburgh Penguins, who featured one of the game's premier players—Mario Lemieux. Lemieux had haunted the Rangers many times with his terrific offensive play.

There was going to be no Stanley Cup for disappointed Rangers fans that year. The Penguins defeated the Rangers, 4-2. It was a summer of reflection for this maligned hockey franchise. Many had thought the Rangers would be serious contenders for the Stanley Cup with Messier on the team. It proved to the fans and to management that New York needed to have more talented players on the roster than just Mark Messier.

*Eyeing the puck, Mark Messier tries to break away from Ron Francis of the Pittsburgh Penguins. Though the Rangers had the best record during the 1991–92 regular season, the Penguins were able to defeat them in the second round of the playoffs.*

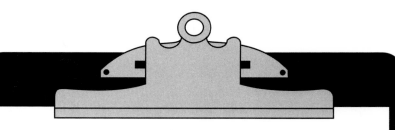

# STATS

The Hart Memorial Trophy is an annual award given to the most valuable player in the NHL. Here is a list of players who have won this award multiple times.

| Player | Times Won |
|---|---|
| Wayne Gretzky | 9 |
| Gordie Howe | 6 |
| Eddie Shore | 4 |
| Bobby Clarke | 3 |
| Howie Morenz | 3 |
| Bobby Orr | 3 |
| Mario Lemieux | 3 |
| Jean Beliveau | 2 |
| Bill Cowley | 2 |
| Phil Esposito | 2 |
| Dominik Hasek | 2 |
| Bobby Hull | 2 |
| Guy Lafleur | 2 |
| **Mark Messier** | 2 |
| Stan Mikita | 2 |
| Nels Stewart | 2 |

The year 1992–93 was going to lead to even more disappointment for the Rangers and Messier. Messier did play in his one thousandth NHL game on April 7 at New Jersey and tied a career high with a 6-point game against the Pittsburgh Penguins on November 25. However, the season was a disaster; the Rangers failed to make the playoffs. The chants of "Nineteen forty" started to surface at arenas around the NHL other than just the Nassau Coliseum, when the Rangers were in town. The echoes of the chants were even becoming more aggravating to Messier. "I hear the fans chant '1940, 1940' in Washington, on Long Island, everywhere," he said. "I don't want to hear it anymore after this season."[2]

For that to happen, the Rangers were going to have to win the Stanley Cup, or the chants were going to get even more frequent and louder. Messier was also going to have to back up his words. He was going to have to show the way for the other Rangers. During the first two seasons, fans were expecting the Rangers to perform better with Messier. It didn't happen. Rangers fans were becoming skeptical now. Messier started to hear frustration from the fans, most of whom had never seen the Stanley Cup carried around Madison Square Garden.

"I think he's more motivated to win here than he was the last few years in Edmonton, if that's possible," said teammate Kevin Lowe, who also had played as an Oiler with Messier. "Mark made it his mission to win a Cup in Edmonton after Wayne left, but I see a more determined Mark Messier here. I think he wants to win it here because he would love to see the people of New York respond to us winning the Stanley Cup."[3]

Words had to be translated into action if the Rangers were to win the Cup. The Rangers hired Coach Mike Keenan to have a man with a steady hand behind the bench for the 1993–94 regular season. It worked. New York finished first overall in the NHL, with 112 points. This would give the Rangers much-needed home-ice advantage in the playoffs. The Rangers' first-round opponents were the hated Islanders. For so many years the Islanders had beaten up on the Rangers. The Islanders won four straight Stanley Cups, 1980–83, while Rangers fans were forced to watch losing hockey. This embarrassed many longtime Rangers fans, who hadn't seen a Cup for fifty-four years. The chants of "Nineteen forty" rarely surfaced during this series. The Rangers smashed the Islanders in four straight games.

Their second-round opponent was supposed to be tougher. The Washington Capitals had always played the Rangers tough. But New York was different this year. Messier and company blasted the Caps in five games. If Washington was tough, then the New Jersey Devils were an even bigger problem. It was Messier's bold statement before Game 6 and Stephane Matteau's overtime goal in Game 7 against the Devils at Madison Square Garden that lifted the Rangers into the Stanley Cup Finals against the Vancouver Canucks.

There was excitement in New York City for the first time in many decades when hockey was discussed. Could the Messiah, Mark Messier, lead the Rangers to the promised land? Messier knew there was still some unfinished business. He was glad that the Rangers fans were happy to be in the finals. But winning the Cup was the only goal he cared to think about.

Vancouver stunned the Rangers in Game 1 by winning in overtime on the Rangers' home ice. But New York bounced back in Games 2, 3, and 4, winning all three. It appeared that the Rangers were ready to grab the Stanley Cup on their home ice in Game 5. Before a roaring crowd thirsty to drink from the Cup, the Rangers disappointed themselves and the fans by losing. To make matters even more tense, New York saw the series tied, 3–3, when the Canucks won Game 6 on their home ice.

*After winning the face-off, Messier looks to beat the St. Louis Blues' Rick Zombo to the puck.*

Would the Rangers again hear the chants of "Nineteen forty" next year? What a horrible thought: The Rangers might lose Game 7. After all, the Rangers had a 3-1 advantage at one point during the series.

A crowd of 18,200 gathered at Madison Square Garden on June 14, 1994. This date would be remembered no matter what the outcome of the game. The Rangers wanted to score first, since the Canucks had scored first in the last four games. New York wanted to get its home crowd into the game early, so scoring the first goal was very important. The Canucks' Pavel Bure was the first player to have a serious scoring opportunity. Bure's quick wrist shot was steered aside easily by New York goaltender Mike Richter. The Rangers fans appeared to relax after that scare.

The Canucks continued to press the Rangers' goal. There was a flurry in front, with several Rangers and Canucks standing together just five feet in front of Richter. Out of the pack came two shots by the Canucks. Both were stopped again by Richter. The Rangers did not have many scoring opportunities early in the first period. Messier's first shot was pushed aside by Vancouver goalie Kirk McLean. Rangers winger Steve Larmer's windup shot glanced off McLean's left glove, falling just wide of the net. Now it appeared that the Rangers were gaining some momentum.

Rangers defenseman Brian Leetch picked up the puck by his net. He moved slowly, then quickly, around two Canucks as he approached the red line. Leetch snapped a pass off the right boards toward a streaking Messier, who was challenged physically by a Canuck, but slipped past the Vancouver player along the boards. Messier picked up the puck by the boards and crossed over the blue line. He eyed McLean, but if he had shot, it would have been a difficult chance since he was at a sharp angle. Messier then started skating toward the center. He stickhandled past another Canuck. The crowd started to roar, sensing something special might happen. Messier looked around to see what his best option was—shoot or pass. He spotted defenseman Sergei Zubov circling around his right side and heading toward the net. Messier made a beautiful behind-the-back pass to Zubov, who quickly passed it to Leetch standing to the left of McLean. Leetch fired and scored. Rangers led, 1-0! The crowd roared at the Garden. Messier and Leetch celebrated by hugging each other. Messier had now scored a point in twenty-one of twenty-three Rangers playoff games, but he and the Rangers weren't interested in individual achievements. They had only the Cup on their minds.

The Rangers continued to forecheck and to work hard trying to get the puck along the boards. Their hard work paid off. Referee Terry Gregson called Jyrki Lumme of the Canucks for holding. This gave the Rangers a power play and a one-man advantage. Keenan immediately sent out Messier's line for more offense. Shots by Leetch and Alexei Kovalev were stopped by McLean, but the pressure from the Rangers power play continued to mount.

Kovalev moved across the left side and had Adam Graves in the middle. Messier was stationed on the right of Graves. Kovalev passed to Graves, who shot quickly. Goal! The Rangers now led, 2-0! The crowd roared louder as Messier, Kovalev, and Graves came together as one to share a hug.

Messier and the Rangers realized they could not relax. There was still plenty of time remaining. The Canucks' Greg Adams came speeding down the center toward Richter. Adams shot, and the puck slipped through Richter, but it dribbled wide of the net. New York still led, 2-0. The first period ended with the Rangers holding that advantage, but there were still forty more minutes of hockey to be played.

In the second period, the Canucks started to mount some offensive pressure on Richter. With

Gregson about to call a penalty on the Rangers, the Canucks' Trevor Linden picked up a bouncing puck near center ice. He immediately turned himself around and sped toward the Rangers' net. With Leetch trying to hold him up from behind, Linden moved around the defenseman and chipped the puck over Richter's shoulder and into the net. Goal! The Canucks had now pulled to within one goal of the Rangers.

Messier knew the Rangers could not have a lapse here. He shouted to his teammates to forget about it and play even harder. New York began to mount its own offensive attack. The Rangers' hard work along the boards led to another penalty on the Canucks. The crowd started to roar in anticipation of something happening for the Rangers. For so many years, Messier had excelled on the power play. Rangers winger Brian Noonan skated toward the Canucks net and tried to pass to Graves, who was standing about two feet directly in front of McLean. The Canucks defenseman had Graves pinned, so Noonan's pass deflected off of Graves and away from the pile in front.

Noonan regained the puck and took a shot toward McLean. The puck was stopped in front, but Messier, standing quietly to the right of McLean, reached out with his stick and slapped at it. "Goal!" the crowd roared, as Messier swung his arms skyward when the light went on behind the Canucks' cage to signify a score. The Rangers now led, 3-1. The Rangers maintained that advantage going into the third period. Just twenty more minutes, and the Rangers would end their long Stanley Cup drought.

The Canucks were not going to give up. Their determination was the main reason why they were in the Finals. To make the situation even more tense for the Rangers, one of their best defensemen, Jeff Beukeboom, was not available for the last period due to an injury. The Rangers pressured the Canucks early in the third period. McLean made some great saves to keep the score at 3-1. Noonan was robbed twice in front of McLean, who stuck out his leg both times to stop a potential goal.

The Canucks started to pressure as well. Bure intercepted a Rangers pass and darted between the Rangers' defense. When he was about to get off a shot, Esa Tikkanen dragged Bure down in front of Richter. A penalty was called on the Rangers. Linden soon converted a pass for a goal. The Rangers now led, 3-2, and a lot of hearts started racing at Madison Square Garden. There were still fourteen minutes remaining in the game.

With the score so close, Messier was now going to be called upon by Keenan to take more face-offs and play more. New York came close to regaining the two-goal advantage when defenseman Kevin Lowe's slap shot banged off the goalpost. Noonan's close-range shot was stopped again by McLean. It was apparent that it was going to be difficult to score again on McLean, so it was important that the Rangers play well defensively.

The Canucks almost tied the score when a Vancouver shot struck the Rangers' goalpost too. The action was now becoming quicker and more furious. The minutes were ticking away. Six minutes left, five minutes left, four minutes left. . . . As each second ticked away, the roar of the crowd was escalating higher. Three minutes remained . . . two minutes were left . . . the crowd at MSG was now standing and shouting encouragement to Messier and the Rangers.

The Canucks continued to press with just 1:34 left. Vancouver called time-out to rest their star, Pavel Bure. But this also enabled the Rangers to rest Messier and Leetch. A shot by the Canucks was blocked in front by Messier. One minute was now left. Vancouver pulled McLean out of the net for another skater. The puck deflected up in the stands . . . 37.8 seconds left. The Canucks continued to press. Bure's shot was stopped in front . . . 1.1 seconds remained!

Messier and the Rangers were now ready to

carry the Cup around the Garden. The puck was dropped for the face-off. The puck deflected behind the Rangers net. The Rangers won! The Rangers won! The drought was over! Fireworks exploded inside the fabled arena in New York City as the Rangers mobbed and hugged each other. People outside the Garden were jumping around and shouting. Messier and Keenan hugged each other at center ice. The crowd was deafening.

The glitter of the Stanley Cup could be seen from a distance. It was being carried up the runway for the Rangers to claim. NHL commissioner Gary Bettman called Messier over to claim the Cup. Messier's hands hoisted the Cup high as the Ranger fans roared. Many fans had tears in their eyes as Messier swung toward the boards so the fans could have a better look at the Cup. Messier looked up in the stands to spot his family. He said, "I can't believe it." The crowd roared more as Messier flashed a huge grin and handed the Cup to Kevin Lowe, who took the Cup for a spin. "The Messiah has delivered," said MSG TV announcer Sam Rosen, referring to Messier's leadership.

The Rangers celebration culminated in a parade that was viewed by over one million people. The cheers continued for Messier and the Rangers in 1994–95, but New York would not be able to defend

*Messier celebrates winning the Stanley Cup, by raising it up for the New York fans. In 1994, the Rangers won their first championship since 1940, and Madison Square Garden was in a state of pandemonium.*

the Cup successfully. After stunning Quebec (now Colorado, the Cup winner in 1995–96) in the first round, the Rangers lost four straight to Philadelphia.

Messier and the Rangers also did not fare well in 1995–96. The Rangers came from behind to beat the Montreal Canadiens in the first round, but an old foe—the Pittsburgh Penguins—again eliminated New York from the playoffs. After the 1995–96 season was over, Messier had only one thought: to regain the Stanley Cup.

## FACT

Mark Messier keeps in good shape during the off-season by water-skiing, swimming, and sailing at his estate on Hilton Head Island, South Carolina, which includes a guest house that can sleep sixteen people, tennis courts, a swimming pool, and a gym. He also enjoys running on the beach and playing golf with his family.

# Chapter 6

# The Reunion

**F**or so many years, Mark Messier and Wayne Gretzky formed one of hockey's most feared duos. Gretzky became a free agent after the 1995–96 season. The St. Louis Blues, for whom Gretzky played during that season, tried very hard to re-sign the fast centerman. But Messier made it clear to the Rangers management and their fans that signing Gretzky would be the best thing for the New York hockey team.

Rangers management listened very closely, and when the Vancouver Canucks withdrew from the race to sign Gretzky, the Rangers emerged as the team that Gretzky liked the most. Rangers General Manager Neil Smith also wanted to make sure that getting Gretzky would be in the best interests of New York.

First, it has to make hockey sense," Smith said. "After that, you have to see if it makes financial sense and third, there's an indescribable return on the investment when you have the players like [Mark Messier] Mess, [Wayne Gretzky] Gretz, and [Mario Lemieux, Penguins] Lemieux. We've seen how Mark has elevated this franchise and that has paid dividends financially. . . . if people get excited going to games or watching MSG or Fox, it's a benefit down the road."[1]

Messier had built his reputation by smashing through opponents, while Gretzky had polished his superstar label with his pretty passes and his lightning-quick reflexes. The Rangers made their offer to Gretzky after the Canucks dropped out and it was apparent the Blues weren't going to make a big-money offer to him. It didn't take long for Gretzky to accept the offer from the Rangers. Now Messier and Gretzky, heroes from the Edmonton Oilers' Stanley Cup years, were reunited.

"From a selfish standpoint, I'm happy for Wayne to be here," Messier said. "I'm happy because it's going to be competitive. We're adding a guy I don't think we've had since I've been in New York. Offense is something we've been missing on and off the past few years."[2]

## FACT

When Mark Messier first began playing for the Edmonton Oilers, he copied one of Wayne Gretzky's habits. Before a game, he would eat a grilled cheese sandwich and lots of french fries smothered in ketchup.

*Mark Messier and Wayne Gretzky won four Stanley Cups together as members of the Edmonton Oilers. In 1996, Gretzky signed a free-agent contract with the Rangers reuniting the former teammates.*

Messier was right. Gretzky will help improve the Rangers offense. For the past couple of years, there has been a lot of pressure on Messier to lead the New York offense. Every night, Messier has found two, sometimes three players surrounding him. It eventually wore down the physically conditioned Messier late in the 1995–96 season.

"They've been the most dynamic duo in hockey," Blues general manager and coach Mike Keenan said. "He's not the Wayne Gretzky of 10 years ago but he's still a great hockey player. Wayne is still a 100-point man."[3]

Gretzky, born January 26, 1961, in Brantford, Ontario, still carries a lethal offensive stick even at the age of thirty-six. He finished the 1995–96 season with 23 goals and 79 assists for 112 points. Not bad for any hockey player. "There's still only a handful of guys that can score as many points as he can," Messier said. "Can our team use 120 points? How many players can put up 110 points?"[4]

This was the greatest reflection on Mark Messier. In today's sports society, athletes showboat for television cameras, beg for media attention, and whine about their salaries. Messier highlighted the advantages the Rangers would have when they signed Gretzky. Messier showed that he always puts the team first and himself second. "For me and him at

**FACT**

When Messier won the Hart Trophy in 1990 as the NHL's Most Valuable Player, he took it away from his friend Wayne Gretzky, who had won it nine of the previous ten years.

*Messier hits Bill Houlder of the Tampa Bay Lightning with a bone-crushing bodycheck that almost sends him out of the rink. Part of being a team captain is sacrificing yourself for the good of the team.*

this point in our careers, it's definitely about trying to win," Messier said. "Championships now for myself and him are more important now. We can retire and live a good life. . . . There's no question in my mind he wants to play in a place that gives him the opportunity to win."[5]

Gretzky holds single-season records for goals, assists, and points. He scored 92 goals in 1981–82. He had 163 assists in 1985–86 and 215 points the same season. He holds the career mark for goals, with 837 coming into the 1996–97 season. But beyond the statistics is the desire, like Messier's, to win another Stanley Cup.

The Rangers signed Gretzky for two years, hoping that both he and Mark Messier would rekindle the same excitement they created in Edmonton. Both Messier and Gretzky were older now—more than ten years older. They certainly couldn't be expected to produce the same kind of numbers they did when they were twenty-five years old, but they were going to try. Captain Messier helped wash away some anguished moments in Rangers history by leading New York to the Stanley Cup in 1994.

Rangers fans believed that Messier and Gretzky would lead the Rangers to another Cup before both decided to call it quits. "No one deserves a better opportunity than Wayne," Keenan said. "Hopefully,

*Mark Messier shows the Stanley Cup trophy to the fans at New York's Yankee Stadium.*

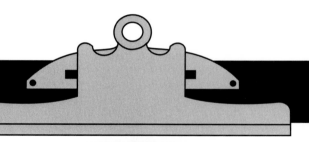

# STATS

Mark Messier is one of the greatest hockey players of all time. He ranks in the top ten in all three major offensive categories. (Through 1999–2000 season.)

## Most Points

| Player | Points | Player | Points |
|---|---|---|---|
| 1. Wayne Gretzky | 2,857 | 6. Steve Yzerman | 1,562 |
| 2. Gordie Howe | 1,850 | 7. Ron Francis | 1,560 |
| 3. Marcel Dionne | 1,771 | 8. Paul Coffey | 1,528 |
| 4. **Mark Messier** | 1,714 | 9. Ray Bourque | 1,521 |
| 5. Phil Esposito | 1,590 | 10. Mario Lemieux | 1,494 |

## Most Goals

| Player | Goals | Player | Goals |
|---|---|---|---|
| 1. Wayne Gretzky | 894 | 6. **Mark Messier** | 627 |
| 2. Gordie Howe | 801 | 6. Steve Yzerman | 627 |
| 3. Marcel Dionne | 731 | 8. Mario Lemieux | 613 |
| 4. Phil Esposito | 717 | 9. Bobby Hull | 610 |
| 5. Mike Gartner | 708 | 9. Brett Hull | 610 |

## Most Assists

| Player | Assists | Player | Assists |
|---|---|---|---|
| 1. Wayne Gretzky | 1,963 | 6. Gordie Howe | 1,049 |
| 2. Paul Coffey | 1,131 | 7. Marcel Dionne | 1,040 |
| 3. Ray Bourque | 1,118 | 8. Steve Yzerman | 935 |
| 4. **Mark Messier** | 1,087 | 9. Stan Mikita | 926 |
| 5. Ron Francis | 1,086 | 10. Larry Murphy | 911 |

it'll work out for him . . . I think he'll be able to share the responsibility of becoming a lead player with Mark [Messier]. There's no better place for him to go and share that responsibility. He spoke quite a bit about Mark when he left St. Louis."[6]

With Messier and Gretzky together again the Rangers were confident going into the 1996–97 season. The team finished fourth in the Atlantic Division, with a record of 38–34–10. The Rangers defeated the Florida Panthers and the New Jersey Devils to advance to the Eastern Conference Finals. Injuries to some of the Rangers' key players began to take their toll, and the Rangers were defeated by the Philadelphia Flyers, 4–1.

After the season, Messier had a contract dispute with the Rangers' management. He decided to leave, signing a three-year contract with the Vancouver Canucks worth an estimated $20 million. After his three years in Vancouver, Messier re-signed with the Rangers in 2000. Resuming his role as captain, Messier hopes to lead New York back to the playoffs.

# Chapter Notes

## Chapter 2

1. Austin Murphy, "The Look of a Winner," *Sports Illustrated*, May 9, 1988, p. 53.

2. Interview with Stan Fishler, *Inside Sports*, November 1987.

3. Chris Smith, "On Your Mark," *New York Magazine*, May 4, 1992.

4. Ibid.

5. John Feinstein, "On Balance, He Is the Best," *Sports Illustrated*, February 21, 1983, p. 55.

6. Ibid.

7. Murphy, p. 54.

8. Jim Matheson, "A Maturing Messier: Star on the Rise," *The Sporting News*, December 17, 1984, p. 40.

9. Feinstein, p. 55.

10. Ibid.

11. Interview with Stan Fishler.

## Chapter 3

1. Cam Cole, "Oilers Found Blueprint to Beat Isles," *The Edmonton Journal*, May 20, 1984, p. Cup 6.

2. Jim Matheson, "Messier Lit the Fuse for the Oilers," *The Edmonton Journal*, May 20, 1984, p. Cup 6.

3. Ibid.

4. Jim Matheson, "Oilers Quench an Old Thirst," *The Edmonton Journal*, May 20, 1984, p. Cup 2.

5. Jim Matheson, "Oilers 'Still the One,'" *The Edmonton Journal*, June 1, 1987, p. SC 2.

6. Ibid.

## Chapter 4

1. Jim Matheson, "Cup No. 4, How Sweet It Is," *The Edmonton Journal*, May 27, 1985, p. 52.

2. Austin Murphy, "The Look of a Winner," *Sports Illustrated*, May 9, 1988, p. 52.

3. Jim Matheson, *The Sporting News*, December 11, 1989, p. 43.

4. *The Sporting News*, December 4, 1989, p. 41.

5. Ray Turchansky, "Snapshots of Champions," *The Edmonton Journal*, May 23, 1990, p. D3.

6. Larry Wigge, "There's a Scare in Messier's Glare," *The Sporting News*, June 11, 1980, p. 35.

7. Ibid.

8. Jim Matheson, "Emerging from Gretzky's Long Shadow," *The Sporting News*, December 11, 1989, p. 43.

## Chapter 5

1. Stan and Shirley Fishler, "Messier and Messier," *Village Voice*, April 6, 1993, pp. 148, 150.

2. Larry Wigge, "Mark His Words: The Cup Stops Here," *The Sporting News*, May 16, 1994, pp. 51–52.

3. Ibid., p. 52.

## Chapter 6

1. Laura Price, "Rangers in Driver's Seat for Gretzky's Services," *Newsday*, July 20, 1996, p. A3.

2. Laura Price, "My Last Stop," *Newsday*, July 22, 1996, p. A41.

3. Laura Price, "Mess O'Gretz," *Newsday*, July 21, 1996, p. B3.

4. Laura Price, "Great One Expectations," *Newsday*, July 19, 1996, p. A61.

5. Ibid.

6. Laura Price, "Keenan Has Blues," *Newsday*, July 21, 1996, p. B26.

# Career Statistics

| Season | Team | League | GP | G | A | PTS | PIM |
|--------|------|--------|-----|-----|------|------|------|
| 1977–78 | Portland | WHL | — | — | — | — | — |
| 1978–79 | Indianapolis | WHL | 5 | 0 | 0 | 0 | 0 |
| 1979–80 | Cincinnati | WHL | 47 | 1 | 10 | 11 | 58 |
| | Houston | CHL | 4 | 0 | 3 | 3 | 4 |
| | Edmonton | NHL | 75 | 12 | 21 | 33 | 120 |
| 1980–81 | Edmonton | NHL | 72 | 23 | 40 | 63 | 102 |
| 1981–82 | Edmonton | NHL | 78 | 50 | 38 | 88 | 119 |
| 1982–83 | Edmonton | NHL | 77 | 48 | 58 | 106 | 72 |
| 1983–84 | Edmonton | NHL | 73 | 37 | 64 | 101 | 165 |
| 1984–85 | Edmonton | NHL | 55 | 23 | 31 | 54 | 57 |
| 1985–86 | Edmonton | NHL | 63 | 35 | 49 | 84 | 68 |
| 1986–87 | Edmonton | NHL | 77 | 37 | 70 | 107 | 73 |
| 1987–88 | Edmonton | NHL | 77 | 37 | 74 | 111 | 103 |
| 1988–89 | Edmonton | NHL | 72 | 33 | 61 | 94 | 130 |
| 1989–90 | Edmonton | NHL | 79 | 45 | 84 | 129 | 79 |
| 1990–91 | Edmonton | NHL | 53 | 12 | 52 | 64 | 34 |
| 1991–92 | Rangers | NHL | 79 | 35 | 72 | 107 | 76 |
| 1992–93 | Rangers | NHL | 75 | 25 | 66 | 91 | 72 |
| 1993–94 | Rangers | NHL | 76 | 26 | 58 | 84 | 76 |
| 1994–95 | Rangers | NHL | 46 | 14 | 39 | 53 | 40 |
| 1995–96 | Rangers | NHL | 74 | 47 | 52 | 99 | 122 |
| 1996–97 | Rangers | NHL | 71 | 36 | 48 | 84 | 88 |
| 1997–98 | Vancouver | NHL | 82 | 22 | 38 | 60 | 58 |
| 1998–99 | Vancouver | NHL | 59 | 13 | 35 | 48 | 33 |
| 1999–00 | Vancouver | NHL | 66 | 17 | 37 | 54 | 30 |
| **NHL Totals** | | | 1,479 | 627 | 1,087 | 1,714 | 1,717 |

# Where to Write
# Mark Messier

Mr. Mark Messier
c/o New York Rangers
2 Penn Plaza
14th Floor
New York, NY 10121

## On the Internet at:

*Official NHL Web Site*

<http://www.nhl.com/lineups/player/8449573.html>

*ESPN Profile Page*

<http://espn.go.com/nhl/profiles/profile/0010.html>

# Index

## A

Adams, Greg, 77
All-Star Games, 33–35, 65
Anderson, Glenn, 11, 13, 16, 50, 60

## B

Beliveau, Jean, 70
Bettman, Gary, 81
Beukebook, Jeff, 79
Bossy, Mike, 13, 39
Boston Bruins, 48, 54–57, 60–61
Bourque, Ray, 54, 92
*Boys on the Bus, The,* 49
Brodeur, Martin, 10, 14–18
Bure, Pavel, 75, 79–80

## C

Calgary Flames, 35
Campbell Conference Finals, 46
Canada Cup, 53, 63
Carpenter, Bobby, 56, 61
Central Hockey League, 30
Chicago Blackhawks, 46
Ciccarelli, Dino, 92
Cincinnati Stingers, 28
Clarke, Bobby, 70
Coffey, Paul, 13, 47, 49, 65, 92
Colorado Rockies, 25
Conn Smythe Trophy, 43–44
Cowley, Bill, 70
Craven, Murray, 49

## D

Dea, Jack, 21
Detroit Red Wings, 60

Dionne, Marcel, 92

## E

Edmonton Oilers, 14, 29–33, 35, 37–40, 42–43, 45–51, 54–65
Esposito, Phil, 70, 92

## F

Francis, Ron, 69, 92
Fraser, Barry, 40
Fraser, Kerry, 12, 15–16
Froese, Bob, 47
Fuhr, Grant, 49

## G

Gartner, Mike, 92
Gillies, Clark, 35
Goring, Butch, 39
Graves, Adam, 77–78
Gregson, Terry, 77–78
Gretzky, Wayne, 13, 33–34, 42–43, 49, 57–59, 61–64, 70, 85–88, 90, 92–93

## H

Hart Trophy, 63, 70, 88
Hawerchuk, Dale, 92
Hextall, Ron, 50
Houlder, Bill, 89
Houston Apollos, 30
Howe, Gordy, 60, 70, 92
Hull, Bobby, 92

## I

Indianapolis Racers, 26, 28

## J

Jones, Janet, 57

## K

Keenan, Mike 12, 14, 51, 72, 77, 79, 81, 88, 93
Kovalev, Alexei, 14–16, 77
Kurri, Jari, 13, 42, 50, 92

## L

Lafleur, Guy, 70
Larmer, Steve, 12, 75
Leetch, Brian, 10, 15–16, 76–78, 80
Lemieux, Claude, 9
Lemieux, Mario, 68, 70, 86, 92
Lidster, Doug, 18
Lindbergh, Pelle, 47
Linden, Trevor, 78–79
Linseman, Ken, 42
Los Angeles Kings, 33, 41, 57
Lowe, Kevin, 58, 63, 72, 80–81
Lumme, Jyrki, 77

## M

Mateau, Stephane, 73
McCammon, Bob, 59
McClain, John, 18
McClean, Kirk, 75–80
Melanson, Rollie, 42–43
Messier, Doug, 21–22, 24–26
Messier, Jennifer, 22
Messier Management International, 26
Messier, Mark
    awards and honors, 43–44, 63, 70, 92
    birth, 22
    childhood and youth, 21–28
    draft (NHL), 29

family, 21–27
    NHL career, 7–19, 29–35, 37–43, 45–51, 53–65, 67–69, 71–83, 85–92
Messier, Mary Jean, 24–26
Messier, Mary Kay, 22, 24–27
Mikita, Stan, 70, 92
Montreal Canadiens, 35, 47, 83
Moog, Andy, 60
Morenz, Howie, 70
Morrow, Darrell, 26
Muckler, John, 63
Murdoch, Murray, 21, 23, 68
Murphy, Joe, 61
Murray, Bill, 32

## N

National Hockey League (NHL), 28–33, 35, 37, 39, 59, 68
Nemchinov, Sergei, 10
New Jersey Devils, 7–12, 14–18, 68, 73
New York Islanders, 35, 39, 40, 42–43, 67, 72
New York Post, 7
New York Rangers, 7–19, 64–65, 67–69, 71–73, 75–83, 85–88, 90, 93
Nicholls, Bernie, 8, 12
Niedermayer, Scott, 10, 12
Nilsson, Kent, 50
Noonan, Brian, 78–80
Number Eleven, 26
Nystrom, Bobby, 39

## O

Orr, Bobby, 55, 70

## P

Philadelphia Flyers, 31, 45–51, 83

Pittsburgh Penguins, 68–69, 71, 83

Playfair, Larry, 41

Portland Buckaroos, 22

Potvin, Denis, 35, 43

## R

Richter, Mike, 8, 10, 12, 14–16, 18, 75, 77–79

Rosen, Sam, 81

## S

St. Louis Blues, 74, 85

Sather, Glenn, 29–33, 38, 55, 63

Shore, Eddie, 70

Simpson, Craig, 60

Smith, Billy, 35, 40, 42

Smith, Neil, 85–86

Smith, Steve, 61

Spruce Grove Mets, 24

Stanley Cup Playoffs, 7–12, 14–19, 33, 35, 39–40, 42–43, 45, 47–50, 54–55, 57–62, 64, 68–69, 72–73, 75–81, 83

Stewart, Nels, 70

## T

Tampa Bay Lightning, 89

Tikkanen, Esa, 11, 79

Tocchet, Rick, 51

Trottier, Bryan, 35, 43, 92

## V

Vancouver Canucks, 58–59, 73, 75–81, 85

## W

Washington Capitals, 72

Western Hockey Association, 22

Winnipeg Jets, 45

World Hockey Association, 26, 28–29